The Calm After Your Storm
Power to be Whole Again

by

Taniesha Richardson-Wiley, MPH

The Calm After Your Storm
Copyright © 2019
Taniesha Richardson-Wiley, MPH

ALL RIGHTS RESERVED
No part of this publication may be reproduced, stored in any electronic system, or transmitted in any form or by any means, electronic, mechanical, photocopy, recording, or otherwise without written permission from the author. Brief quotations may be used in literary reviews.

All Scripture quotations are obtained from the King James Version and Life Application Bibles, unless otherwise noted.

ISBN-13: 978-0692870761
ISBN-10: 0692870768

FOR INFORMATION, CONTACT:
Taniesha L. Richardson-Wiley, MPH
InfiniteMelodies3@aol.com

Printed in the USA by:
Amazon Kindle Direct Publishing
Images Printing

Disclaimer

Although I am a public health professional, I do not profess to offer medical or psychological advice. The content in this book comes from the depths of my "imperfect self", and the words on these pages are merely based on my subjective experiences and faith in God. As you read this book, I hope that you are inspired, encouraged, and have comfort in knowing that with God, you will survive the toughest storms through not only your faith, but also fellowship with others and prayer.

Acknowledgements

I would like to dedicate this to all who survived the greatest challenges and obstacles while on this journey called life. I hope that this will encourage you to persevere and succeed in all endeavors. I dedicate this to my beautiful family- Primarily, to my beautiful daughter, Destiny Ariana, my handsome son, Kyler Thomas and supportive husband, Kevin; to my parents, Terica and Jackie, Sr. and to my siblings and their families- Jacqueline/John, Jackie Jr./Jada, Tiffany/Roderick, and Terrance; and to all my wonderful friends and associates who have made a difference in my life while on this journey! Each of you contributed to where I am today and I am grateful for you all:

D. Campbell, Z. Harris, J. Silverman, D. Nelson, D. Miller, T. Williams, T. Walls, M. Sanders, R. Sanders, J. Thomas, B. Thomas, C. Hartaway, M. Simpson, L. Smith, S. Johnson, S. Croom-Riley, L. Lehing, J. Holden (RIP), C. Roland, L. Humphries, S. Couch, B. Hager, T. Mitchell, L. Scott; A. Rose, J. Jones, CDC- P. McLean, K. Collins, W. Heirdt; A. Mattison, J. Richter, M. Williams, Mama Jackson, Mama and Papa Langston (RIP), B. Noble, E. Northrop, The entire Richardson Family, The Jagers Family, The Cooper Family, The Harris Family, The Ridgway Family, The Mitchell Family, The Lee Family, The Dupins Family, The Love Family, The Washington Family, The Mobley Family, The Wilbert Family, The Townsend Family; J. McGregory, Auntie Jean, C. Jones, J. Elliott, N. Parrish, Little Seven, Aunt Phyllis, Mama Johnson, C. Johnson (Johnson's Montessori), J. Byers, B. Bohanna, A. Alcorn, T. Steele; The MWD, the GGMBC Ministries-including the Youth and Sister to Sister Ministries; and to all of my OES Sisters- special thanks to Sis. Lindsey, Sis. Fisher, and Sis. Bradley; to all of my Sorors of Delta Sigma Theta Sorority, Inc.- special thanks to G. Perez, L. Rogers, T. Henson, K. Crow, M. Norwood, K. Merritt, and all of my line sisters from Lambda Upsilon, Spring 1996. Never forgotten: Grandmother, Cynthia, Mother, Grandma Sister, Terrance, Auntie Virgie.

A Special Thank You

I would like to take the time to give a special "Thank You" to the individuals who gave me a solid foundation and support beyond measure- my beautiful parents, Jackie Sr., and Terica Richardson. I would like to take the time to say, "Thank You" for always being there for me. You offered encouragement and believed that I could succeed. As a child, I always admired your love for each other as well as your love for us; and now I appreciate the discipline and wisdom. When I became an adult, I learned the true essence of survival and living life to the fullest. Through your teachings combined with my experiences, my relationship with God is stronger than before. Many obstacles and trials tried to obscure my way and decelerate progress; but my faith, the prayers of the righteous, and your loving support allowed me to strive harder and achieve unimaginable dreams. My dreams have finally become my authenticity. I often said that if I would have known what I was going to encounter on this side of heaven, I would have given up a long time ago; but because of my relationship with God and all that you instilled in me, I was able to stand and survive the toughest storms. I could not have made it. Every day, I thank God for His Grace and Mercy, and most of all, I thank God for You. Thank you for always being there for me. I love you Mom and Dad!

Life is But a Vapor

"You do not know what will happen tomorrow. For what is your life? It is even a vapor that appears for a little time and then vanishes away".

James 4:14

Introduction: The Calm Before The Storm

The perfect day. The sun is shining and the brisk wind sweeps across your face. The temperature is just right; it is not too hot nor is it too cold. Everyone is smiling and happy. As you walk by them, they smile at you, wave, and then they ask, "How are you today?!" You smile back, wave and respond, "I am great! Today is a good day!" You continue towards a place where you find peace and tranquility (my favorite places were always a coffee shop, music room, or a park). You Inhale. Exhale. Reflect. Smile. Then you say to yourself, "Yes, this is a good day". You later begin to think about the things that matter to you the most. For some people, it is their career or social life; for others, it is their health or family. Every person in your life is doing well. Your career has skyrocketed to heights beyond that which you could ever imagine. You are stable and free from worries. Life is good. Your family is good, and all is well on this day and at this moment. You wish that you could bottle this moment and pause the time. As you leave your happy place and journey to the next destination, you look around and noticed that the atmosphere changed. You looked up and noticed clouds gathering. The wind blows stronger. Your cell phone rings, and the news crush you. Your life begins to spiral from a happy place to a state of sadness, fear, and gloom. You begin to wonder, "what happened to my sunshiny day when life was calm and everything was good?!"

Storm \ˈstȯrm \

NOUN. A disturbance of the atmosphere marked by wind and usually by rain, snow, hail, sleet, or thunder and lightning; a serious disturbance; VERB. To blow with violence, to attack by storm, to be in rage, a disturbed or agitated state; **synonyms:** attack, assail, assault, bombard, disturb.

Calm [kä(l)m]

NOUN the absence of violent or confrontational activity within a place or group. "the elections proceeded in an atmosphere of relative calm" · **synonyms:** tranquility · stillness · calmness · quiet quietness · the absence of wind. "in the center of the storm calm prevailed" **synonyms:** stillness · tranquility · calm · calmness · lull · silence ·

Chapter 1

The Outpour

Romans 5:3-4 "...but we also rejoice in our sufferings, because we know that suffering produces perseverance; perseverance, character; and character, hope."

"I'm sorry…there is no heartbeat…I am very sorry. You can either come in this evening or we can take him tomorrow", said the doctor on March 21, 2008. Through disbelief, shock, and tears, we embraced and briefly discussed our options. We slowly whispered, "We will come back tonight…". Just "yesterday" his heartbeat was so strong and he was growing as scheduled. What happened? That day forever changed my life. That was the hardest and longest ride home.

We notified our families and packed for the evening to deliver our 4½ month old baby boy. We headed to the hospital in silence and tears. I prayed that it was not true; I prayed that that we would arrive at the hospital to find out that our baby boy was just in the wrong position, and that the doctor would find his heartbeat. I prayed that I would continue to feel him moving or even kick. I prayed. I hoped. I prayed again, but the outcome was still the same. It was all true- My firstborn baby boy died.

As the time passed, I remember how our families were right there supporting us. I remember looking at their faces as each of them stood in the room before I went to deliver him. Their hearts were heavy and they felt our pain. I tried to be strong and reflect the image that I would get through this storm. Moments after they left the room, I cried and felt like I failed… again. Family comforted and ensured me that it was not my fault. They reassured me that we were going to get through this together. As the evening progressed, I was prepped to deliver our son, and the medication made me very drowsy and weak. I remember seeing my mom standing on one side- holding my hand and saying that my hands were cold; and baby boy's father standing on the other side. I remembered waiting for the doctor, but she never showed up. The nurse and my baby boy's father delivered him. Tiny enough to hold in one hand was a beautiful, breathless baby boy.

My son. Our son. We named him Darian which means "Gift". He had all fingers and toes. He looked like he was just sleeping- peacefully. I held him in my hands as long as I could. I smiled. I cried. The tears did not stop flowing. I was weak. I remember giving Darian back to the nurse. If I could hold him forever, I would have. Then everything became a blur. I could hear chatter and chaos. Another nurse came in the room. I remember hearing her say that I needed to have surgery immediately. The nurse talked to Darian's father about signing papers. I heard panic in his voice as he asked questions for clarity, but there was no time. He signed them, and I was rushed into the operating room. As the surgeon began to count down, I saw a white light...and it felt like I was floating in a dream. For that moment, I had no worries and was at peace. It felt like a safe place to be. What seemed like only minutes were hours; and when I woke up, I was back to reality--in a recovery room. This experience changed my life forever.

Days after my release from the hospital, we had a ceremony to celebrate and remember Darian. Many friends and family flocked to the church. This showed us how much they truly cared about my family. They stopped by the house to visit; called and sent many cards and gifts. Then there came a time that the visits declined, and people had to go on with their lives. It was at this time that I would sit alone wondering what happened to my sunshiny yesterday, when things were considered normal and life was good? When the "noise" ended, and when everyone went back to their daily routines, there was a "loud silence". Reality hit harder than before, and I felt like I failed. I remember screaming, crying and asking God "WHY". I did everything right, WHY did my baby die?

My angel baby was tiny and perfect in my sight; asleep forever- never to wake up…never to see or experience life on this side of heaven. The tears continued to flow, and I questioned God.

Response: Nothing.

"This is so cruel! What did I do to deserve this? I followed Your commands; I'm not perfect, but I strived to live for you; why was my baby taken away from me?! From us?!" "What happened??!"

Response: Nothing.

Over the course of time, I could not bounce back, and it was very difficult to move forward. Months after our loss, Darian's father expressed that he was no longer happy in our marriage and moved out of our home. During that season, I lost my son and his father- my husband. Every night I cried myself to sleep, waking up throughout the night; pacing the floor and looking out of the kitchen window with hopes that he would pull up any moment, and walk through the door. I whispered through my tears, "God, WHY is this happening to me? I prayed every day for my marriage, for us; please answer me. I seek your guidance, so speak to me; order my steps and help me to understand all of this".

Response: Nothing.

During this season of "whys" and "silence, I had many questions about loss. I lost a grandmother, my baby and my husband's heart all in one year. I had so many questions- especially about my baby boy's death. To have the ability to carry a child is a blessing; but to carry and lose a child is the worse pain ever. No one should EVER feel this pain. I will never understand why I was given the ability to feel Darian growing inside of my womb- the most beautiful feeling ever- to later hold my breathless baby boy and lay him to rest before he could experience the beauty of life.

I was healthy, young, and happy when I realized that I was going to be a mommy. I followed the instructions that were given to me by my doctor. When I first found out that I was pregnant, I did not know that I had a uterine fibroid. I went for an annual exam EVERY YEAR, and the tests never revealed fibroids. I am no expert, but I did some research and according to the Mayo Clinic, a uterine fibroid is a *noncancerous growth that appears in women of childbearing years; it is not associated with an increased risk of cancer; they range in size from seedlings-undetectable to masses. These masses can distort or enlarge the uterus. Fibroids usually do not interfere with getting pregnant, but it is possible that it could cause infertility or pregnancy loss. Fibroids raise the risk of pregnancy complications, such as placental abruption, fetal growth restriction and preterm delivery.* The fibroid grew with Darian. Before we lost him, we noticed very little fluid around our baby boy on the ultrasound, but his heartbeat was strong. I was given a prescription; told to rest and was sent to a high-risk doctor for further testing later that week. When we finally made it to the high-risk doctor, he did another ultrasound, and that is when we found out that there was no heartbeat.

Although there was a period of loneliness and silence, a few people would say that everything was going to be okay. I wanted things to be the way that they were. I wanted my marriage to be strong, and I wanted my baby boy, but God's plans for my life were different than what I imagined or planned.

One day, my mom and I had a heart to heart talk. My parents never interfered with my personal life, but gave sound advice if they were asked. On this day she asked, "did you know that we almost lost you?". We then talked about my marriage and she said, "You must let him go…he is not coming back; get yourself together and move on". I said, "But mom…". She stated firmly but sweetly, "Let. Him. Go". This was hard, because I loved hard. I was so accustomed to "fixing things" and being in control. This was something that I personally could not fix or control.

Life was not easy, but looking back, I have a clearer understanding of my destiny. These losses were life-changing encounters, and my experiences tried to "break" me or shatter my faith. Although I was broken within, I walked around with the comfort in knowing that everything was going to be okay.

One day, as I walked on a river trail alone, a still small voice whispered, "Trust Me". A cool breeze swept across my face, and I heard those words again, so calming…so soothing, "Just Trust Me". I suddenly felt peace. It was "peace" that I had not felt in a long time. As I exhaled, my burdens began to feel a little lighter. I said, "Yes…yes. I will trust You". It was at that moment, that I felt "a calm" concerning Darian.

Every time I feel a cool breeze sweeping across my face, I call it an "Angel Kiss" from heaven; sent as a reminder that I am never alone on this journey. No, I do not understand the "why's", and I'm not sure if I ever will; but, I will continue to trust the process and work on my well-being. I will continue moving forward, realizing that God's plan is better than my own. With every passing moment, I made the choice to Trust Him more than ever, and this has made the difference!

Always in My Heart: Mommy's Angel Baby
My Thoughts TO You, My Angel Baby:

The thought of you brought so much joy and made us all smile-
We were happy and so proud although it was for a little while.
We began to prepare for your arrival- just a few months away-
So much to do in so little time, but realized you could not stay.
We looked forward to holding you; giving kisses everyday-
We looked forward to watching you grow, as you ran and played.
We wanted to teach you right from wrong, to tell you about someone nice-
Someone who could save your soul, His name was Jesus Christ.
God saw fit to take you, although I often asked why;
He said you are playing in Heaven's park, on clouds in the sky.
I was sad, upset, and mad when you were taken away from me;
It was too soon- you did not even have time to fulfill your destiny.
But, God has been a comforter and let me know that you are fine-
Angel kids and cousins are playing with you;
and your great grands are treating you kind.

You have so many loved ones who are now in heaven with you,
So, now I know that you are in good hands,
My sweet baby boy, you are always in my heart; rest in love, and know that Mommy will see you again.

My Thoughts FROM You:

Mommy, mommy, don't you cry Yes, I am doing great!
God is taking great care of me-
there's nothing but love and not a bit of hate.
I saw the world and the condition it's in,
but mommy please stay strong;
Know that I am doing well,
and know that you did nothing wrong.
I saw your tears and felt your pain when you held me close to your heart;
Never will we say good-bye; never will we part.
Stay strong and always believe- that God will see you through;
Even through the toughest days, believe that He will do-
Exactly what He said He would- never will He leave you comfortless;
For we know that all things work together for the good…according to His purpose and righteousness.
Take care and hold your head up high; know that you, too, are missed-
Just know that every now and then,
I will send an angel kiss.
When the breeze comes across your face- it is to let you know that everything will be okay;
We will see each other again- on that great and beautiful day!

Written By: Taniesha

Chapter 2

The Quiet Storm

"He who dwells in the secret place of the Most High shall abide under the shadow of the Almighty. I will say of the Lord, He is my refuge and my fortress; My God, in Him I will trust." 91 Psalms 1-2 NKJV.

Eight years from the time Darian died, my family encountered another devastating storm- this one was a quiet storm. On January 14, 2016, I picked up my pen again after many years to finish writing this book. I started reviewing my manuscript, when I received a call from my baby sister. She said that my baby brother had not made it to work (which was very unusual). She left her job to see if he was okay. She later called back and said that he was in the ER at one of our local hospitals. I told her to keep me posted and that I would be there as soon as I could. I made it to the hospital after work. From that moment and 6 days after, our lives changed forever. A quiet storm approached. This was one of the strongest storms that EVER hit our family. No words. So unexpected. So UNREAL.

My family lost an amazingly, talented link in our family. He was my baby brother, my parent's son, and to those who knew him, a friend. He was in a car accident, and this tragedy changed our lives forever. It was without warning. We prayed for my brother, and we believed that he would be totally healed on THIS SIDE of heaven. We rejoiced in advance for a supernatural healing and miracle. Death NEVER crossed our minds, because our faith was so strong that my baby brother would pull through. THIS PAIN was the worst pain yet and cut to the core. My brother had so much life and purpose here. We did NOT want him to leave us. We wanted him back with us.

Earlier on the day that he passed away, I saw a vision of my baby brother walking on a road. He came to the fork in that road; he saw God in front of him, with His arms opened wide. God then gave my brother a glimpse of heaven. My brother looked back and saw all of us behind him. He saw us praying that he would come back to us and crying that he would stay. He did not say a word, but he smiled and gave us a look that reassured us that he was going to be better in the arms of God. He gave us the "Peace" sign and walked towards God.

Later that day, I remember singing "Conquerors" in the hospital chapel along with my baby sister and other brother. We left the chapel, hopeful that he would get better. Our family has seen miracles, and we just knew that this would be another one. We then received the news that he died. My brother received his heavenly wings. He is now safely resting in the arms of God. We miss him, and this was an extremely difficult time in our lives. I had many questions for God, because, as I stated, we all believed in His healing power. We prayed- believing and trusting God to heal my brother; to make him "whole" again. Then I asked, and this may sound crazy, but was my brother's death God's way of giving him a brand new life? Was that "the healing"- to no longer have to worry about sickness or earthly pain? Did my brother really have a glimpse of his brand new life in heaven? Why couldn't the doctors that God put on this earth save him? These questions may sound crazy, but yes, as a strong believer in God, whose faith is unwavering, I had those questions. Moreover, I decided that it was okay to ask questions.

One day, I was really struggling with loss, and missing my brother. We connected through music. My baby brother played the drums, my sister and I played the keyboard/piano and my other brother would sing. I started thinking of good memories that we as a family shared and was a total mess, because I missed those moments. Later that day, I reached out to my cousin who has a gift of working with families who have lost loved ones. I asked her how to get through this darkness. She redirected me back to my faith in God and reminded me that this is not the end. She reminded me that my brother was 'saved' (in my faith, being saved means to accept Christ into our hearts- believing that Christ died on the cross for our sins, that He rose and is now in heaven with God. The ordinance is baptism and the Lord's supper to commemorate what Christ did for us). She said that it was okay to weep, but not to weep as if there was no hope. That was my comfort for that moment, and I needed to hear that right then. I had a flashback of when I ministered to others through music, when they lost loved ones. Music was also "my" comfort. My friends, you must seek your comfort. It is okay to cry when you are missing your loved one. It is okay to scream. Find a healthy way to release and find the comfort to get through your storm. It is also imperative that you take care of yourself.

Even now, the messages and posts on my brother's social media page give me peace and comfort. He posted quotes that appeared on my timeline as memories during the times that I really needed it. Posts like, "Everything is going to be OKAY", "DO LIFE", or my favorite one, "FINISH EMPTY".

My brother brought a host of people together at the time of his death under one setting; and I know that he was smiling to see such a fellowship and gathering of people he loved from all races and creeds. Everyone gathered to celebrate his life. His memorial service was amazing and beautiful. My brother "finished empty". He was not perfect- none of us are perfect- but he gave his all in everything he did. He fulfilled his purpose. He headed towards an ultimate 'peace' and 'calm' place- No more storms, but eternal rest until Christ returns. I can only imagine no more pain or sorrow- just sunshine and cool breezes every day!

Now it is up to everyone impacted by his life to carry out his dreams and fulfill his legacy. What was his dream? My brother enjoyed helping others. He also enjoyed music and capturing beauty through the lens. He took beautiful photos of nature, and captured wonderful memories of families and friends. He enjoyed mentoring and helping youth as well as his peers-, encouraging them and giving them hope that they can achieve their dreams, if they believed and worked towards them. Right before he passed away, he wrote a phrase on his social media page. That phrase was Dream. Believe. Work. To honor our brother, we launched the Terrance Richardson (T. Rich) Dream Believe Work Foundation, Inc., in which we offer mentorship sessions to youth and young adults. Older adults can also participate, because we realize that everyone could use a mentor.

We held fun sessions that focused on life skills- equipping everyone with the tools that they need to survive.

I want to encourage you to also "finish empty". What does that mean? It means to give your all in everything you do. Do not give up when the storms come. Even through life's storms- the obvious, boisterous ones and even the quiet ones, persevere and continue to press your way towards your destiny. Make a positive impact on someone else's life. Know your purpose and pursue your dreams. LIVE. When you have given your all- positively influencing the lives of others and living yours to the fullest; when your work here on earth is done, and when God calls us to our eternal home in glory, we can truly say that we have finished empty.

Chapter 3

When There Are No Words

"Trust in the Lord with all your heart and lean not on your own understanding; in all your ways acknowledge Him, and He will make your paths straight". Proverbs 3:5-6, NIV.

I always believed this- during God's silence, He sends people along the way to encourage you and to let you know that everything will be okay. So many people are not sure what to say to those of us who have lost a child or a loved one. The secret? LISTEN. Most of the time, we just want someone to listen. Only God can fix what was broken. No one can repair our broken hearts nor could they give us our loved ones back. While going through my grieving process, I did not want advice or solutions, I just wanted someone to listen. As a listener, please try to avoid saying that you understand what a person is going through especially if you have never been through it. Just be prepared to listen and allow people the ability to express how they feel. Let them talk, cry, or even scream if they want to.

You can also pray for them. Pray that God gives them the strength to get through these tough times. Another wonderful thing that you could do is take the mourning person out. Take them shopping, to the park, out to eat, or to a place that they like or enjoy. I will never forget being taken to the park and out to eat. It was a change of scenery, and I could breathe again. For those few hours, my mind was not on my grief. I even smiled again and was reassured that a host of people was there for me.

I also attended a support group meeting and a ceremony to remember Darian. I highly encourage you to do your research regarding certain support groups that may be best for you. You never want to leave worse than you came! As a family, we attended a recommended grief support group meeting. It appeared that the instructor was still "healing" from their loss that occurred over 15-20 years ago, and it came through during the session. My dad was encouraging the instructor more than they were helping us. We left feeling worse, "drained" and more hurt than we did before we arrived! After that, we were very careful of the invitations we received or answered to. Then one day, my family received an invitation from my brother's friends and their family. It was a grief retreat, and we traveled to Texas as a family. This is what our family needed. We are a very spiritual family, but we are still human. We always comforted others during their time of need, but needed someone to pour something into our spirits that will get us through this challenging time. Never over it- just through it. During this retreat, and this may sound weird to you, but I felt my brother's presence there. His spirit was with us. It was comforting. We were away from distractions, and it was in a place that he would have loved. This retreat offered what we needed and we are now "Living Forward". A lot of what I shared in this chapter, was gained from my experience there. Nothing will ever replace that hole or emptiness that we feel inside, but it will help you through it, so find a credible place that specializes in grief counseling. The weight from the grief will be lifted from your heart, because your loved one who passed away would have wanted that. They would want you to live forward. They live through you when YOU LIVE. I encourage you to live so that their life and legacy lives through you.

As a friend to the griever or grieving family, always keep them in your thoughts and prayers. And just remember to avoid saying things that are insensitive. Some very insensitive phrases that you should avoid include: "Get over it" or "you're not over that yet?", "It's not like you're never going to see them again", "Move on with your life", "Don't cry", "Stop crying", You're crying again", "Get yourself together and stop with the pity parties". I have heard and seen it all. THESE WORDS HURT. From my experiences, grieving people do not want to hear that, because they miss their loved one at that moment and want to hold them here and now. Sometimes it is best not to say anything when you have no words to say. You cannot "fix" the way that they feel, but you can give support to the person who has experienced loss.

Again, the best thing to do is just listen unless they ask you for advice or for a response. Pause. Then ask them if they want to be consoled or hugged. A hug goes a long way, but it is all in timing...their timing. I remember the day that my brother died, a person came up to me, grabbed me and began hugging me and crying harder than me! This made me feel worse! At that moment, I did not want anyone else around me. I just wanted to be with my immediate family. During the retreat, we were in groups and after our assignments; the people in our groups would ask if we wanted a hug. It was more welcoming when they asked to enter my space. Some people may not want to be held or touched, so always ask.

Yes, we will always wonder, "what in the world happened?!" We never imagined that we would be at this place and state. To those who lost a child, sibling, I can truly say, "I can relate- I have been there". However, if you have never experienced such loss, avoid saying that you can relate when you cannot. This is also insensitive. As a person who experienced grief, it was important to me who I allowed in my personal space. Some people mean well, but sadly, there are others who find pleasure in watching you suffer or cry. Avoid being around people like this.

I will never forget sitting in my quiet place one day when a person I knew entered through my door. Everyone who knew my family, heard about my brother. This person also knew that my brother was in an accident and died. I looked up as they approached where I sat and began talking about their weekend. The person shared how blessed they were that their spouse was still alive after being in an accident. I was not bothered about the testimony; but was annoyed by the great details that were shared about their spouse's accident. And then, to make matters worse, this person stated that they could only imagine what my brother went through. Really? It was like that person wanted a reaction from me. After they saw that I was not going to "break", the individual left my presence. I just thank God that even through that, He guarded my heart and kept me from reacting negatively.

If a person cannot listen, pray for you, or hold you up through your grief process, they do not need to be in your space;

and you have the right to dismiss them without feeling bad about it. This is your journey, and a devoted friend or person that means well would understand this. As mentioned, when there are no words to say, just listen and continue to pray for them.

As the person on the receiving end of comfort, it is also important that you pray that God sends the right person or people your way and guard your heart. Spend quality time with Him to hear HIS voice. When there is emptiness or loneliness, instead of using that quiet time to hear clear answers or directions, we often search for advice from others or comfort in things as the first option instead of seeking God to send the right people. This action invites unnecessary "noise" into our lives. When there is a lot of "noise", no one can clearly hear anything; and there is difficulty in distinguishing God's voice from the sounds of the world. We then begin listening to only what others may say instead of hearing what God is trying to tell us. Imagine talking on a cell phone while a train passes by. You began to yell to the person on the other end, and they are steadily saying "what" or "I can't hear you". It is the same way with God. You must remove yourself from the noise and into a quiet place to clearly hear God's voice. You will then begin to discern if the people surrounding you are sent by God. The person that entered my space clearly was not sent by God. And because I stay in God's presence, I was able to recognize it, and I allowed God to protect my heart and bridle my tongue from lashing out.

Sometimes, I wish that I could fix the broken pieces of those who have experienced loss. I pray that, in those lonely nights- when memories of your loved one who has transitioned cross your mind- you remember the happy times. You feel their presence and smile again through God's love. Know that they are always with you…

I believe that God sometimes sends us signs to let us know that they are with us. My brother was an artist- a drummer and an inspiring photographer. One 'early evening', right before sunset, I felt the wind blowing (angel kisses), heard thunder while birds chirped and saw lightening in the distance. To me, this was peculiar, because all of this occurred at the same time. It symbolized something meaningful to me that gave me peace. The lightening in the distance represented my brother's heavenly "camera flash", and the thunder represented his "drums". A tear dropped, and I smiled. For that moment, I was comforted, because I felt my brother's presence, and remembered that he is always with us. So, every time I see beautiful clouds in the sky, a beautiful sunrise or sunset, or even a rainbow after a rainy day, I am comforted and reminded that my brother is with me always. The beautiful skies and clouds; sunrises and sunsets are his canvases from heaven- reminding us that he is always with us. He is and will forever be in our hearts. Always.

Chapter 4

In the Time of Trouble

Psalm 46:1-3 NIV "God is our refuge and strength, an ever-present help in trouble. Therefore, we will not fear, though the earth give way and the mountains fall in to the heart of the sea, though its waters roar and foam and the mountains quake with their surging"

During the darkest storms, we sometimes search for relief to make the pain go away right then. Many people lose their minds at this point of their storm or fall into a "rebellious" state- letting the "debris" consume them. It was at this point of my storm that I sought comfort in people who I felt understood what I was going through. It was comfort that I vulnerably accepted which later turned into a boisterous whirlwind…

Over the course of time, I began to open up about my trials and struggles. I was rescued from the world's issues. I had a friend who was there for me, who comforted me and told me that everything would be okay. He had to go away for a while; and in the meantime, I became more involved in my church and the community. While staying busy helping others, I met more people. One person had a sense of humor, a lot of energy and excitement! We would laugh for hours about the craziest things! It had been a long time since I smiled or laughed. The more we talked, the more I realized that we were going through the same thing. I began to enjoy life again. I yearned for peace with no pressures, but then I became very comfortable and unguarded…

Be careful when you become too comfortable and be watchful. The enemy knows your weaknesses and will paint a picture to make anything look good. I was free and nothing bothered me or could hurt me again. My life changed again forever. I wanted a family. I was in my mid-30's and had so many mixed emotions. I had a love child and knew that I had to be healthy- physically, mentally, and emotionally. During those nine months, I had my moments of ups and downs, but for the most part, the father and my family were there. They were very supportive, even during the delivery. The events were videoed from the time that I was getting ready to head to the hospital to the time I delivered. My family stayed by my side. The pregnancy went without any problems or complications. I was happy to carry and deliver a baby to its fullest term. Holding my beautiful baby girl, Destiny, in my arms was priceless.

All that I desired was a family and thought that this was it. After a year, there was no commitment and I found myself broken again. My heart ached…again, and my smile turned into tears…again. I would never bash anyone for their actions, because people will show you who they really are in time. It was up to me how I responded. I did some soul searching and realized that it was best that I moved on—alone—with my daughter. That was a very interesting "season" in my life, and I grew from that point. From every situation I encountered, I learned lessons and applied those lessons to my life. The biggest lesson that I learned was that if you pray and surrender everything to God, or if you ask God to show you what you need to see about a person, you must be ready for it. You must ask yourself the question, "Is this worth it"? or "Is this something that I want to deal with- FOREVER"?

I knew that God had something in store for me if I just returned to Him, and I was right- He did! I remained totally focused on God not giving into distractions or temptations again.

This was for my "heart's sake" as well as for my daughter. It was a trying time, but a "much needed" time to reflect, regroup and get back on the path that God laid for me. I began to focus on my whole well-being- spiritually, mentally, physically, and emotionally. It made a difference in my life, and that's when doors began to open.

The only way that a person can get through such devastation in times of trouble is by having an anchor and taking shelter. Your anchor is your support system- there to hold you down during the storm and your shelter is God. He will protect you if you remain in Him. I thank God daily for guiding me through that storm. If I did not have God in my life and a wonderful family as well as a few supportive friends, I am not sure how I would have made it through that difficult time. The lesson during this phase in my life is this, and I encourage all ladies- Know your worth and be true to yourself! Ultimately, and I have stated this before, you must know that there is comfort in God during your darkest hours; and if you just trust Him and stay connected to Him, you will be able to cope with it anything! He will give you strength that you never knew you had. You will also be able to help so many people by letting them know that God will bring them through any situation if they only believed and trusted Him. You must first believe this before you can convince someone else to believe it. Now, we are getting ready to launch deeper on how to be the best YOU that you can be, and receive all your heart's desires. It worked for me, so let's go!

Here are the things that I must Let Go of:

_____

_____

_____

_____

_____

_____

_____

_____

_____

_____

_____

_____

_____

_____

_____

_____

_____

_____

Chapter 5

Born Into Greatness

Before I formed you in the womb I knew you, before you were born I set you apart; I appointed you as a prophet to the nations." Jeremiah 1:5

We were born to live; but to only die and live again. Many have said that this is just the cycle or circle of life. It is best to make the most of life while you are here. Although we were born to die, be encouraged, and know that you were born into greatness. It does not matter how you were born, you must believe and know that you were designed to be great! As you move forward, truly understand who you are and why you act, think, or speak the way that you do. This chapter is very simple- you were created to be just the person you are, and as mentioned, it is important to first understand who you are. Let me repeat this: from the time you were conceived, you were born into greatness. Before you were even thought of, God had a purpose for your life. Sometimes our atmosphere or surroundings can "shape us" into who we are- whether positive or negative. If you want to succeed, regardless of your background or your past, it is imperative that you surround yourself around positive people who can help you grow in a healthy and positive way. Connect with successful people who can share how they succeeded. Never let anything or anyone discourage you from being great. You were born to be great, so be great. You have control over your own destiny.

If you experienced hardship or difficulties growing up, you can break any generational misfortunes that exist within your family. You can break negative cycles by not doing the same things that negatively affected you and the people surrounding you. For example, we were designed to live prosperously.

Although your ancestors may have struggled, you do not have to struggle. You may say, "It is easier said than done" or "life happens" or "That is just life- welcome to reality". You may also believe that we will struggle regardless and will never totally have an abundance; or you may even become content because "as long as your bills are paid and you still have on your lights, water, gas on as well as a home, that is just enough!" Nothing is wrong with this way of thinking, but aren't you ready to receive an *overflow* of blessings?

Even in these perilous times, we can still prosper- financially, physically and spiritually. You must see yourself where you really want to be, believe that you can get there and then work towards it. Nevertheless, you must deal with issues that may have prevented you from reaching your fullest potential. You have to acknowledge those issues first in order to deal with them. Then connect with people who can help you. Identify the resources that will help you get to the next level. God will send help, if you really want it. He always does. Once help arrives, utilize it and start living life abundantly that God has designed just for you!

If you are already experiencing an overflow, share with others *how* you got there. I thank God for people I connected with over the years- especially at work. I always surrounded myself around positive people who were successful and knowledgeable. I always wanted to learn more, so I took what I learned from them and applied that knowledge and skills to be successful. I am STILL learning. I also want to encourage you- never stop learning. If you stop learning, you stop growing. My work village showed me how to be the best professional I could be, and God 'advanced' me. I thank them every chance that I get, because I knew that God sent them my way. I strived to plant in others the things sown in my life. I wanted to see everyone succeed. Some said "thank you", while others went on their way- which was fine, too. I received joy knowing that they received it and advanced to levels that they never knew existed. So, two things here- #1 sow into someone else's life; and #2 if someone sows into your life, remember to say thank you or show your appreciation. This is just common courtesy- even though the person who planted into your life is not looking for anything in return. They just want to see you succeed.

    So, as mentioned, surround yourself around positive people. Do not allow the negative aspects of your past overtake you in the present. Acknowledge that you can experience God's overflow if you work towards it. Every morning, acknowledge that you are blessed to see another day, look in the mirror at the beautiful person you are, embrace your uniqueness, make great things happen and touch someone else's life.

"For if you give, you will get! Your gift will return to you in full and overflowing measure, pressed down, shaken together to make room for more, and running over. Whatever measure you use to give—large or small—will be used to measure what is given back to you". Luke 6:38, TLB.

My Beautiful Attributes:

Chapter 6

True To You – Remove the Mask

I Peter 3:3-4, NIV. "Your beauty should not come from outward adornment, such as braided hair and the wearing of gold jewelry and fine clothes. Instead, it should be that of your inner self, the unfading beauty of a gentle and quiet spirit, which is of great worth in God's sight."

True beauty genuinely comes from within, and whatever is within will eventually reveal itself outwardly. Sometimes, we get caught up in society's definition of beauty. We think that we must look or appear a certain way to be accepted—plastic or cosmetic surgery is on the rise; implants to enhance certain areas of the body are steadily increasing; liposuctions and tummy tucks are popular among both men and women. Cosmetic corporations will forever remain in business- mascara, face powder, eye liner, blush, eye shadow, lip gloss, lip stick, lip liner, finger nail polish- you name it, almost every woman has it! Personally, I LOVE getting "dolled up", and this has become an "almost-everyday" thing. It makes me feel good! Another major thing that I have often dealt with over the years was my weight. I did not realize until I entered adulthood that yo-yo diets or not eating much- which was common as a cheerleader for 4 years- never worked. Over the years, I felt good about myself, but strived harder to lose weight and keep it off, however, I gained more than I lost.

My physical appearance meant a lot to me, but I did not realize until this phase of my adult life that for many years, I covered up flaws- hiding behind a mask, and I gained weight to hide behind pain. It was difficult embracing being overweight. Internally, I was not happy, and I felt that I let God down by not taking care of His temple- which was my body. After I had my daughter, I totally focused on God's plan for my life when it came to my appearance. I began to focus on the things that were healthy for me, and made the decision to live a healthy lifestyle-eating healthy and exercising. I had to realize that I had to love myself first by taking care of the temple God blessed me with. I wanted to run and play with my daughter at the park. Most of all, I wanted to live and see her grow up without being sick or ill. I made the decision that I would live a healthy, happy life.

Many times, people use things to enhance their features or cover up flaws; to feel good or impress other people. We often seek acceptance and think that these things define who we are as a person, but does it? Does this truly define who we are? Only what is on the inside of us—our internal makeup—our temple, defines who we are. If you were to remove your mask, how would you genuinely appear to yourself? How would others view you? Would you care how you appeared to others? In my own personal experience or observation, make-up covered scars, and sometimes A LOT of it is needed, so that no one can see the damage underneath.

Many people want to be free, but are too ashamed of how they would look to the world if they removed the mask. Healing will not take place until we deal with these internal issues and remove the mask of fear and being exposed. Know that regardless of your past hurts, mess-ups, faults, suffering and pain, you can get back up again. However, you must trust God enough to help you along the way. Understand that sometimes He places people along your path to help you. He sometimes works through others to reach you. He also may send people your way that are able to not only reach you, but to help or provide you with resources you may need during that time. The alarming question is what do you do while you are going THROUGH? The pain hurts deeply- internally, emotionally, and sometimes physically. We are so programmed to mask or cover up those emotions; or to be tough and never let people see you down and out. So many times, we have been programmed to put on this mask and smile sweetly; but I have learned as I matured that sometimes it is okay to let others know that you are not a SUPER human! It is perfectly ok not to be perfect. You are just a human being with feelings and emotions too! When we feel overwhelmed, we must not doubt God's ability to bring us out of our overwhelming state. Furthermore, our trials are just testimonies that will not only strengthen us, but also help someone else.

    I did not realize this until I felt like I lost everything. I felt that my inner essence left when I lost my baby boy. I felt like I failed when my first marriage did not work out or when I could not pay my bills- sitting in the dark because my electricity, gas or water were turned off; or the time when I almost lost my home and car. The struggle was unbelievably real. When you lose something or someone that you love so dearly, it does something to the inner being and it hurts. Many people never knew of these struggles. When we share our story, we discover that so many other people have been through the same things- if not more. We then begin to share how God brought us through that storm which in turn, comforts others to know that He will bring them out of their storms too. If we share how we survived, we touch others and give them the comfort and assurance that they need to also survive. It is all in His timing.

The key to survival is to first acknowledge the scars and wounds that you have covered up for so many years. You have covered up past hurts and guilt; putting on so much "makeup" that you have forgotten how you once looked beneath it all. God wants to give you a "makeover"! He wants to give you a facial and a deep cleanse-removing all "impurities" that have damaged you! The mask must come off so that God can repair you. He is the one that can fix what is broken within You must face who you really are to be free again.

It may be unattractive at first, but once the healing takes place, you will look like you once did before the damage occurred. You must be ready to accept the fact that it is a process that takes patience and time. At the end of that process, you will be restored and free- casting all guilt and hurt into the sea of forgetfulness! You will not only be more beautiful than ever before, but also stronger and wiser!

After the repairing phase, there is maintenance. God has given you all that you need to maintain the "best you" and that is His word. Utilize the skills and abilities as well as the power that He has given you to keep that which has been restored. You need that to survive. The enemy will try to come and make you doubt who you are. It will try to give you a mirror to try and convince you that you have not really changed. It will try to bring up past flaws or remind you of the past hurt and pain. Whenever that comes, face it, and say that I will NOT be shackled by the pain that had me bound. I WILL be free! I DECLARE victory- in the Name of Jesus! Understand that the enemy is a LIAR and nothing of it is good. Once you use that God-given power, you can then move forward. Old things have passed away, and all things have become new. You are a new person now. Keep your eyes focused on the price God has for you. It will be well worth the journey.

Set a goal and stick to your "start date". Remember, that you are going through transformation and change will not occur overnight. This is a process, and now is the best time to start. If you 've already started and gotten off track, it is never too late to begin again! Keep resetting if you must, but never give up. By this time next year, you will be a new being, but you must start today.

What Are Your Transformation Goals?

_____

_____

_____

_____

_____

Therefore, if anyone is in Christ, he is a new creation; old things have passed away; behold, all things have become new"
II Corinthians 5:17, NKJV.

Chapter 7

Moving Forward

Always remember this: Two are better than one...if either fall, one can help the other up...a cord of three strands is not quickly broken. Ecclesiastes 4: 9, 10,12NIV.

You cannot move forward until you love yourself! How can you love anyone else if you do not love yourself first? It is so important that you understand yourself and be very specific with your needs and wants. Make sure that your relationship with God is solid so that you can recognize the one He has prepared for you, and never let him or her go. I have learned so much over the years, and I repeat, whoever is designed for you, as long as God is your foundation, you can make it through anything together. Whatever is not designed by God will not work. It will fail before it begins.

Before marriage, understand that two people with unresolved past issues who bring their baggage of past hurts and insecurities into a new relationship are sabotaging the union before it ever begins. Your issues plus your partner's issues equal a pile of issues- a mountain of past hurts and insecurities.

I am going to be completely transparent with you in this chapter, and thank God for healing me to the place that I can even share it with you. Divorce is a loss. It does not compare to death, but it is still a loss. I never thought in a million years that I would experience it, but I did. That was NOT my choice, because it was supposed to be "for better or worse". We were supposed to work things out- regardless of how bad it may have been for either of us. My ex-husband left after our son's death and 2 days before our 3rd year anniversary. We dated 3 years prior to getting married, so I thought that I knew everything about him. He thought that he knew everything about me, too. I wanted the same time and attention I received when we were dating, and it felt like it went away once we were married. Not only that, I was told that I always needed "validation" from everyone else on the decisions we were supposed to make together. He felt that I no longer trusted his judgment and the decisions he made for us, and that I sought attention from others. He did not realize that I only desired his attention- the attention that he gave me when we first met. Why did that have to change once we became married? He worked hard to support us, but what is the point of working hard if you never spend time together? We could never come to a happy medium; so instead of us working it out, we parted ways. This was also the year that my oldest sister was in a coma and we thought that we were going to lose her. My family traveled to Chicago when we received the news that she was non-responsive after traveling from Japan, connecting in Chicago to go to her home in Virginia. After I returned from my Chicago trip, my husband was gone. I often found myself trying to do everything in my power to make it work, but from my perspective, nothing was ever good enough. We had misunderstandings and misconceptions of many things. It had gotten to the point that we no longer had patience or trust. When I saw that he was not coming back, I moved forward.

  Despite this storm, I had to forgive. Memories will be cherished forever, but I knew that, for my own well-being, the pieces of my shattered life had to be put back together again by the only One who could do this- God. With His guidance and the help from special friends and family that God sent my way, I could finally move forward.

It took me a while to forgive. Not only was it challenging to forgive others for past hurts and/or disappointments, but also challenging to forgive myself. I had to finally realize that, after repentance AND practice, we are forgiven by God, so why is it so hard to forgive ourselves? We must let things go. I repeat, LET IT GO. If your hands are full, how can you receive more? We cannot pick up anything else if we continue to hold on to things we should have gotten rid of a long time ago. Imagine how quickly we can receive the blessings that are designed for us when we let old things go! Get ready and in position to receive what God has for you- but make sure that the next choices you make are in line with His will for your life.

Now, PLEASE understand this, too, God will never bless you with something that belongs to someone else. Ever. Think about it. If I wanted YOUR car; not a car that looks like yours, but YOUR car, do you honestly think that God will give me YOUR car- especially if you still have it? Probably not. Stop praying for something or someone who is with someone else. If they are with you while they are with someone else, what makes you think that they will not be with someone else while they are with you? In addition, if a person treated someone else wrong, and got with you, what makes you think that this person will not treat you the way that they treated others? Open your eyes, so that you can see what is the truth. Open your ears, so that you can hear clearly. If you messed up, learn from that, and don't do it again. Become zero tolerant, and take a good look at yourself. Refocus. Regroup. Move Forward.

Nevertheless, the question remains: How can I love fully or move forward when I still feel empty on the inside and have these weights chained to my feet? Again, You must be healed. Only God can do this and it takes time. It is a process that requires patience and time alone. I remember having surgery- which required being cut. It took 6 weeks before it healed, but the process was unbearable. I had to remove bandages and apply medicine to the wound. The medicine burned, but it healed me. The area where I was cut, later became a scar- which was a reminder of my surgery. The healing process took time and was painful, but after I was healed, I felt so much better!

Many times, people rush into relationships without understanding who **they** really are as an individual or without letting go of past hurts. How do you know that you are healed? You are healed when the feelings of hurt and bitterness no longer exist. You can see an ex or someone (the "scar") that you had an issue with and not have anger towards them. Once you are healed, you can forgive, not complain, and move forward. You can exhale and breathe again. You can walk confidently alone, knowing that God has your best interest at heart. You are comforted in knowing that He is preparing that special someone, made just for you! You know that you are healed when you have taken time alone to hear from God and receive clear directions from Him. Then after you follow His directions for your life, you can confidently move forward.

But listen, it is so easy to have high expectations- and we have that right, however, make sure that you meet or exceed the expectations that you seek in a mate. If you expect a financially stable individual, make sure that your finances are in order. If you expect someone who is healthy and fit, make sure that you are in shape and healthy. It is only fair that you reflect your expectations.

To my single friends, stay in line with God's will for your life to receive the blessings He has for you. When you are out of line, you miss wonderful things. Do not worry about being alone, but use this time to become more healthy-spiritually, physically, and emotionally. God gives us free will to make decisions. But for every decision made there is ALWAYS an outcome- whether good or bad. I cannot emphasize the importance of having a solid personal relationship with God first. Let Him guide you and show you how to love yourself first and then the mate He has for you. If you are spiritually, physically, or emotionally unhealthy, you cannot contribute fully to any relationship or be fully happy. Love God first, and love yourself by eating healthy and participating in physical activities that you enjoy. Once you love God and yourself, then you can love your mate the way that they deserve to be loved. I have learned so much over the years of dating. The biggest lesson learned was to understand that you **cannot** make a person stay or love you if they really don't. If they did, their actions would display how much they truly love you, and they would not leave you- especially during a storm. They will protect you and never leave you exposed to the elements of life. I believe that many times things do not work because God did not join the relationship or put it together. I truly believe in the saying that "you cannot put a seasonal person in a lifetime position". This means that seasonal people are just that- there for a season. Do not waste your time trying to build a life with someone who is not meant to be yours or who is not designed for you. Let it Go. It does not matter how well you dress it up, it is difficult when your foundation is on anything other than God and His Word.

If a relationship failed, move on. As mentioned, pick yourself up, dust yourself off and 'keep it moving'. Believe me, there is someone being prepared just for you who will appreciate the love that you must give and will also love you the way you deserve to be loved. When I came to this conclusion, I could truly exhale and move forward. You can do the same thing too. In the meantime, focus on strengthening your relationship with the source of your strength and becoming a "better you"- spiritually, mentally, and physically. Surround yourself around positivity and hold on. It will be worth the wait.

Do not be misled: bad company corrupts good character."
1 Corinthians 15:33.

To all married couples; those of you who have remarried, and to all who are engaged to be married; surrender your spouse to God and pray for him or her EVERY DAY. This is the only way that it will work. So, how do you know whether God joined you with your spouse? You know when you no longer ask yourself that question. You will no longer ask "Did God do this?" Times will get tough, but just remember, if you prayed for them prior to marriage, never stop after you get married. Remember, your spouse is NOT perfect. They have flaws and so do you! We all have our issues that only God can help us with! Build your marriage on a solid foundation which is God.

I thank God, every day for loving me enough to bless me with a wonderful husband, tailor-made just for me. I "surrendered" him to God. Every day, he leads us in prayer- praying for me, our children, himself, and our families. I also pray for him daily in front of our children. This is the foundation and is done before the day begins. If you do not have God first in the beginning, and/or if your relationship is built on lust and feelings *only*, it will not work. Grow together spiritually by studying God's word together, worshipping together and most of all, praying together.

It is important that you obtain the spiritual tools needed to grow as an individual so that you can contribute spiritually in the relationship or marriage. Make sure that you are equally yoked- meaning, make sure that you are both on the same spiritual path and love God more than anything else. If you love God more than anything, everything else will fall into place. You will not have any problem loving your spouse when you love God first. When you love God, you can run away from temptation and cling to your spouse. You are also able to share things without having issues such as jealousy or insecurities. I must admit, it was very difficult for me to trust again! After what I had been through, I had to allow God to heal me. As mentioned more than once, our spouses are not perfect. In the good times and the bad, through the happy times and the sad, be there for each other. Every morning and night, put your spouse in God's hands and leave them there. Let God lead them. God can do more than you ever could. If they love you, they will listen to God and strive to do the right thing- especially by you. This does not occur overnight, it takes work.

    Next, take heed and understand that the desires of the flesh are real. We are never tempted with the things that we do not like, but we are often faced with our greatest weaknesses; and sometimes the things that were not of God that we did in the past are resurrected to destroy that which God has given us in the present. If we are not guarded, it is so easy to get caught up and distracted. My dad always said that it is best not to flirt with the enemy. You cannot handle this in your own power. It is best not put yourself in a compromising situation. Otherwise, you may be devoured and every good thing about your marriage is destroyed because of our fleshly desires. The statement that the grass is not always greener on the other side stands true. That grass on the other side could destroy you. Literally, you must "water" your own. Ask yourself, "is this quick thrill worth losing everything God has blessed me with?" It is not worth it. Moreover, if you already messed up, repent, move forward and never do it again.

One thing that I can truly say, and this did not occur instantly, I have peace and can truly rest at night without worrying about anything. I truly believe that God takes care of His own and will NEVER leave you blind or in the dark when it comes to your spouse. Whenever things are revealed, be prepared, and handle it. Not with a "vengeance" spirit, but with the mindset to discuss a solution or get counseling. Revenge is not the answer when one messes up. Believe me when I say, let God handle it. He will lead and guide you. Remember, if you love God, the desires of the world that you once had are trumped by the love that God gives you to love your spouse. Worldly desires are temporary. Doing things God's way- and in order results in peace and an AMAZING marriage! Once you do things God's way, all things will fall into place. It will not take long to occur, it can happen suddenly, but you must be in position to hear from God and execute His plan designed for you. When you are under God's umbrella, you can deal with life's greatest challenges. When you do things His way, the spouse that He has prepared just for you will always be there and will have your back no matter what- "for better or worse…"

Lift each other up and treat them as the king and queen that they are! Realize that love never hurts. If you love your spouse, you will do everything in your power not to hurt them. God blessed you with them, so it is your responsibility to take care of each other. Wives, your husband deserves to be treated LIKE A KING! Husbands, your wife deserves to be treated LIKE A QUEEN. NEVER bash or badmouth your spouse to ANYONE- EVER! Lift them up- even if they make you mad. They will make you mad. Regardless of what you have been through with your spouse, never ever belittle or disrespect them by your actions or words. Say pleasant things, and do cordial things for them. It is quite okay to brag on each other. This coupled with your actions will make a "happy spouse"! Remember, your actions speak louder than the words that come from your lips. Show your love. You know exactly what your spouse likes and dislikes. If you know that your spouse does not like you to bother him while he is watching his favorite show, find something to do during that time. That is not the time to discuss issues when you know that this is his time. Men, if you know that your spouse does not like it when you leave the toilet seat up, it is not that difficult to remember to let it down. Those trivial things can turn into unnecessary issues; so, make sure you extinguish the small flames before it becomes a forest fire and destroy your marriage!

Listen to each other. Trials will come, but you can handle it if you keep God in the midst of it. You can handle anything if you stand strong together as one, pray together and dismiss the enemy from trying to destroy what God has blessed. Another thing to do that will make a difference is to take out time for each other- do things together and work together as a team.

It is absolutely nothing wrong to have date night at least once a week or twice a month. It does not take much money or effort to do something special for each other- it is the simple things that make a difference. Date night can range from dinner and a movie to cuddling up on your couch, eating popcorn (or feeding each other) fresh fruit while watching a good movie. Once a couple stops dating and becomes consumed with making a living, they forget to live and the zest that won you over is diminished. Never stop dating. Never stop laughing. Never stop loving. And most of all, never stop living. Enjoy life with the person you vowed to spend the rest of your life with. Keep understanding that that no one is perfect and that we all have our flaws, but love supersedes all our imperfections and faults.

God loves you regardless of your mess-ups, so it should be easy for you to forgive and love regardless of your spouse's flaws. Understand that the enemy does not want you to stay married and will try to tempt you with your greatest weaknesses; no new tactics- especially when there is a blessing in view. You could be very close to receiving what God has for you and your family, and then here comes temptation. The key is recognizing it and not entertaining it. If you resist it, it must flee! Recognize. Resist. RUN! There are consequences to all our actions, so be mindful of that. If you know that you have a problem with alcohol, it would probably be best that you do not go to a bar! Get some help. Recognize. Resist. RUN!

Take care of your physical responsibilities as a spouse. Unless you are ill, this is necessary. This is sacred and a blessing, so enjoy each other and make sure that your spouse is loved in every way. Keep yourself up too! Although our bodies change as we age, you still must take care of yourself.

You may not understand each other at times, and when the enemy comes to try and destroy your marriage, recognize the signs, PRAY for yourself and for your spouse. Speak life into your marriage. If you fill your marriage with the love of God, and cling to each other, there will be no room for anyone or anything to come in between that. Nothing or no one can separate that which God has joined! All of your signs are there while you are dating. Yes, you see their "representative" but if you date long enough, you will capture a glimpse of who that person really is. Again, understand that NO ONE IS PERFECT and you will have problems. But those problems are not too big for God to solve if you both are on the same spiritual path or equally yoked.

Lift your spouse up and when times get tough, remember the things that you loved about them in the very beginning. Remember what made you smile before the problems rise. Protect them. Communicate. with them. Whenever you run into a storm, be each other's covering. You will make it through anything as long as you keep God as the center of your lives.

Great Characteristics of my Mate

_____

The Thing that I Love the Most About My Mate

_____

Chapter 8

Preparing Our Future

"Train a child in the way he should go, and when he is old he will not turn from it." Proverbs 22:6, NIV.

As I reflect on how my parents disciplined my sisters as well as my brothers (and me), I remember how we **thought** at that time that they were "mean" parents. We could never get away with things and they knew when we would skip important parts to a story. We thought, *how did our parents know that?* They knew because they probably had been through it as well!

Parents, raising our child or children can also be a storm. It is important that we understand what we once did in order to understand how to relate and discipline our child or children. We must be honest with our own faults and ourselves first, and let them know EARLY the importance of obedience and respect. Many of our young people today are disobedient and/or disrespectful to their parents or other adults. Why are they this way? Ask yourself, *what am I as a parent doing to ensure that my child obeys me?* If I spend more time away from my child than around her- doing my own thing; or if I spend most of my time hanging out, what should I expect? What are they seeing? Young people today are a lot smarter than any of us were. They are more tech savvy and exposed to much more negativity as well as pressures from the world. They are also very observant. They lose respect especially when we say, "Do as I say, not as I do". They see and hear everything, which is why is it vital that they are exposed to positive things when they are at home or in our presence. As mentioned, they are already exposed to negativity in the world; our homes should be peaceful and safe.

We must live a life that is pleasing to God- especially when raising children and provide them with a safe haven. Growing up, I rarely if EVER heard my parents yelling or fighting each other. I know that they may not have always agreed on everything- that is life, but I never heard them disrespecting each other. My parent's house was and still is considered the "happy house". Peaceful.

So, there are two lessons that I learned from that. The first lesson was through the eyes of a child. Although my parents may have disagreed on something, they never expressed it in front of us. The second lesson that I learned was through my "current eyes" as an adult. Because I was not exposed to that type of expression, I do not like to yell. I always believed that it does not take a whole lot of yelling and screaming to get a point across. Yes, I understand that one must use an authoritative tone when disciplining their child- I do that quite often, BUT it does not take verbal or physical abuse to get a point across. It is okay to disagree on things, but it is even better to have healthy dialogues with possible solutions. No one deserves to be verbally abused or disrespected. I have seen it too many times how an individual publicly disrespects the person (or people) that they claim to love. So think about what we say and how we say it- especially in front of our children. Be an example for your child and handle disagreements during a time when they are not around, such as when they are visiting their grandparent's house, playing outside, or sleeping. Our children can feel what we are going through, so strive to be that positive light for them. It will have a larger impact on their lives once they become of age to make their own sound decisions. I am not saying that anyone is perfect; but know that it is vital that we reflect and instill positive principles in our children EARLY. When they are older, they will remember-especially during the times when they must make decisions. Always remember, our children watch everything that we do. They are like little sponges- absorbing everything that they see and hear. You will sometimes catch them repeating or doing some of the things that we do. You may see that they sometimes impersonate your actions or mimic the words that you say. It is our responsibility as parents to make sure that we are careful and mindful of the things that we say or do around our children. It is still important to live the life that our little children may one day live. Meaning, your children are little "carbon copies" of you. Train them early to be the best that they can be. Expose them to greatness as well as the simple things in life- especially the positive, simple things in life.

I must share my "shrimp" story. Every time I think about it, I laugh because it was such a simple lesson! I will never forget going over to my friend's house before a high school football game. I was a cheerleader and she was on the drill team. She had shrimp and offered it. I responded with a confident "SURE" (although the only seafood I ever had at that time was fish sticks or fish sandwiches from Rally's or McDonald's. Oh, and I once tasted little fried shrimp nuggets from Long John Silvers- which of course, did not require "peeling"). So, we both started eating our shrimp. I picked up that shrimp with confidence and started crunching away! I then turned to my friend and said, "This is good, but why is it so crunchy?" My friend looked at me and started laughing aloud. I was like, "What?" as I continued to "crunch" the shrimp. She shouted while still laughing, "Taniesha, you're supposed to PEEL IT"!! She yelled in the other room to her mom, "Mom, Taniesha is eating the shell!" I was like "OHHH"!! She then showed me how, and my response was, "Wow, this tastes better!" Her mom came into the kitchen, and we all just laughed. Her mom shook her head, and was probably wondering "Lord, help this little country girl!" I am just glad that it was not at a restaurant! To this day, we still laugh about the shrimp story. I dare not blame my parents for not introducing shrimp to me, because we were grateful for the food that we had, and I am now teaching my daughter to be grateful for what she has. But, I also shared this story with my daughter, and as simple as it is, I made a point to share "the proper way to eat shrimp". Now she knows how to eat it when she is in public. This was something I considered as a simple thing in life. So again, be the best parents that you can be, and share something positive and new with your children.

    We all know that evil and negativity fills our world. Our children are exposed to so many external pressures. As adults, we are also faced with trials and pressures of life. However, we have control over our own homes and the energy that we allow to flow therein. Anyone could enter my home, but not everyone was invited. Even as a Christian, you must be mindful of who you allow into your home.

Strive to have a stress-free, peaceful place. This is related not only to your responses to stressors in keeping a peaceful place, but also your physical environment. Remove clutter and understand the importance of having a "clean space". Unbelievably, this also affects the moods and attitudes of your home. I did not realize how important this was until I had several "purging ceremonies". I removed things that were stored away in closets and corners of my rooms. Once those things were removed, I had refreshing energy flowing throughout my home. We strive daily to keep a clean home and new energy flows from room to room. Yes, it is indeed difficult with children, but you can do it with their help. So, let us teach our children the importance of keeping a clean home in addition to providing them with a Christian atmosphere.

Lastly, know that God looks at your heart and your intent while giving your children the tools and discipline that they need in preparation for life. Never forget that they are depending on us. If our ways are in line with God's Will and His way, we will be able to handle any situation that we encounter with our children. It is equally vital that we continue to pray for them DAILY and provide them with the love and discipline that they so deserve and need- especially in this terrible and cruel world. So just remember to teach them early and although they are not perfect and will make mistakes, they will remember your teachings. Keep God as the foundation and your home can stand through the toughest storms and still have peace within it.

As for adults who may not have children, continue to be a light for those who see you. You never know how you might affect their lives. You may be the only positive influence that they have or see. They may even look up to you, just by what they see in you and the energy you give. So, continue to shine your light.

These commandments that I give you today are to be upon your hearts. Impress them on your children. Talk about them when you sit at home and when you walk along the road, when you lie down and when you get up. Deuteronomy 6:6-7NIV

What Will You Impress Upon Children?

_____

_____

_____

_____

_____

_____

_____

Chapter 9

The Island

"Teach us to number our days and recognize how few they are; help us to spend them as we should." Deuteronomy 10:12-13, NIV.

As a child, I often visited my grandmother (Grandma Sister) and grandfather (Paw Paw) on what we called The Island. A lot of my family members had their own experiences of The Island. To some, there were great memories of the green and pink houses. My memories were fond ones. As a child, the road to the island seemed so long. There were small bodies of water and fields that surrounded the island as well as a freeway that ran parallel to the road. Odd, but true! There were often old bikes on the island- one had no seat and flat tires, but we rode it like it was brand new! My sister and cousins had an exciting time playing games and making mud pies. We found creative ways to enjoy ourselves on the island. There was ALWAYS food- enough in the deep freezer to last a year or two!

One of my fondest memories is when we spent the night on the island. I remember hearing the crickets sing at night after the rainstorm, and I kept everyone up until someone made them stop. I cried all night, scared of the chirping crickets, but my grandparents and oldest sister assured me that I was safe. There was no need for me to worry. I remember my grandparents having two beds pushed together to make one king size bed and in this bed, I would snuggle right in the middle where the two beds would meet; cover my head and fall asleep until the morning. When the morning came, we no longer heard the crickets. Grandma Sister and Paw Paw would cook rice and hot dogs which were cut in half and fried in a skillet. The aroma filled the house, and we were well taken care of. We enjoyed playing, eating, and having a good time on the island. Regardless of the night time experience on the island, we had so much fun every time we visited. Great memories.

As an adult, I reflect on those moments on the island as opportunities to grow. It served as a reminder to just appreciate life regardless of where you are or your status. Reflecting and relating it to now, the long road stood for life. Nighttime represented life during our dark hours- afraid, crying and sometimes even alone; the crickets stood for the enemy and distractions; my sister and cousin represented the angels and my grandparents represented God. As long as I was in their presence, I felt safe. Now that I am older, I often use this as a symbol to encourage myself and even others whenever they need encouragement.

Just remember this- things may occur that will try to get you off track or prevent you from enjoying life; however, the way that you handle those things makes the difference. Your response to actions that are beyond your control or your reaction always determines the outcome of any situation that occurs. You have the power to choose to either enjoy yourself or allow those situations or "crickets" to affect you causing you to be miserable and unhappy. Many people often wander through life allowing others to control how they feel. Nevertheless, I want to encourage you to regain your power and enjoy your life. Never forget that life is what you make it out to be.

Your happiness is based on how you react or respond to your greatest challenges, but take note that joy is everlasting. Enjoy life and choose this day to obtain joy. Be happy- regardless of the crickets!

How Will You Obtain Joy and Be Happy?

_____

_____

_____

_____

_____

_____

_____

_____

_____

_____

_____

_____

_____

_____

Chapter 10

Power To Be Whole Again

John 1:12, RSV. But to all who received Him, who believed in His name, He gave power to become children of God." James 5:16, TLB. "Admit your faults to one another and pray for each other so that you may be healed. The earnest prayer of a righteous man has great power and wonderful results.

When you fix your mind and heart on things eternal, you can and will survive the greatest storms and will obtain the power to be whole again. I want to close this last chapter with encouragement and reiteration of key points that are mentioned on the pages of this book.

Believe that things are already looking better for you and your family. The key is to stay connected to God! If you are connected to the Power Source, you will forever have "light" and the victory- even during your suffering. Regardless of the trials that you encounter, be assured that everything will work out in your favor, if you hold on. Continue to speak life over all your trials and believe that it will happen. Now you ask, HOW do we continue to go on even in the darkest hours of our lives? Just as you put in time with your loved one or doing something that you love to do is how you will survive. God seeks your time and promises to never leave you. When God takes something from your grasp, He is not punishing you but preparing you for something greater! You must be ready to receive it, and I guarantee you that it is much greater than you could ever imagine or think!

While working on this book, I was told that in three months, I would no longer have a job after working for 15 years at one agency. That was a storm. Even knowing that, I fully trusted God and knew that there was something even greater in my future. He never failed me. I am still working at the same agency with almost 20 years in, doing what I love.

I am learning more each day how to be patient and allow the Holy Spirit to take total control! Do you know that so many times we miss the blessings that He has for us just because we are impatient and fail to wait on Him? I often think that I would have been so much further on this journey if I was more patient...but through it all, I thank God so much for His grace and for being a God of ANOTHER chance. I can truly say that I am understanding life more through His love for me.

I am in total submission to His Will and have recommitted to doing what He has commanded me to do. I never want to be out of His will! We all have done some things that we know that we were not of God, and we have even had some ungodly thoughts. We may even mess up again, and the enemy makes things look glorious while you are in your mess (of course we never acknowledge it as such while we are in it). However, once the masks are removed and we are faced with TRUTH, that is when God can dwell and work through us. Once you totally commit to Him, there is a purging process that takes place in your life. The chains that had you bound are released and you are free! You can finally breathe again.

Please understand this, the adversary does not want you to be an effective vessel, so it tries to destroy you as well as your integrity. I was talking to my wonderful husband about our society and how we as a people, from all races and creeds are destroying ourselves. Most of us are knowledgeable, but systems are set up so that we are not as productive as we could be. As we drove by Cummins prison while on a trip, we had the discussion on how A LOT of money is funneled to these systems. It is sad, because I am almost certain that brilliant minds are behind prison doors, but the choices that were made resulted in that outcome. It saddens me to know this, but there is still a hope.

There is no sin larger than the next. If you are striving to be the best that you can be, regardless of bad decisions or choices; regardless of where you have been or what you have done, when you have God's favor, your integrity is restored and your life is better than ever before! Your walk is not the same and even your talk is different! Yes, going through the fire is a painful process, but in the end, it will be well worth it. You begin to look better, feel better and your life is never the same. What are you willing to sacrifice for His glory?

I encourage you to expect greatness from your storm! I am so excited and look forward to receiving all that He has for me! In the meantime, I will continue to genuinely smile and do what I have been commissioned to do for His glory; focus on my well-being- spiritually, physically, and emotionally and lift others up. You can do the same! Remember these things and know that there is peace- even in valley experiences. Although we may be broken, we are not beyond repair. Acknowledge that you can depend on God and trust Him. Tap into the power that you must be whole again, and conquer the world! You can do this! The God-given power is in your hands! Utilize it to be the best person you can be and expect greatness.

Lastly, God speaks so clearly to us- whenever we feel alone, we should have comfort and believe that we are never lonely. When we surrender, LISTEN, and FOLLOW His instructions. His Will shall be done on earth as it is in heaven; and everything that we want or desire falls into place. Now, the enemy may put doubt or fear in our minds, and make us think that what God says will not work, but understand that if it is God ordained, it WILL work! As I always say, Trust Him. Trust His process.

Keep Living. Keep Moving. Keep Believing, and knowing that there is a Calm After Your Storm!

Mark 4:39-41, TLB. "Then He rebuked the wind and said to the sea, 'Quiet down! And the wind fell, and there was a great calm! And He asked them, 'Why were you so fearful? Don't you even yet have confidence in Me?' And they were filled with awe and said among themselves, 'Who is this man, that even the winds and seas obey Him?'"

The Calm After Your Storm Scriptures

Allow these scriptures to inspire you as you experience peace and calm after your storm.

Romans 6:5-7, TLB. "For you have become a part of Him, and so you died with Him, so to speak, when He died; and now you share His new life, and shall rise as He did. Your old evil desires were nailed to the cross with Him; that part of you that loves to sin was crushed and fatally wounded, so that your sin-loving body is no longer under sin's control, no longer needs to be a slave to sin; for when you are deadened to sin you are freed from all its allure and its power over you."

John 14:6, "Jesus answered, 'I am the way and the truth and the life. No one comes to the Father except through Me.'"

Hebrews 2:18, TLB. "For since He Himself has now been through suffering and temptation, He knows what it is like when we suffer and are tempted, and He is wonderfully able to help us."

James 1:2-3, TLB. "Dear brothers, is your life full of difficulties and temptations? Then be happy, for when the way is rough, your patience has a chance to grow."

Psalm 90:12, TLB." And now, what does the Lord your God ask of you but to fear the Lord your God, to walk in all His ways, to love Him, to serve the Lord your God with all your heart and with all your soul, and to observe the Lord's commands and decrees that I am giving you today for your own good?"

Hebrews 4:12, TLB. "For whatever God says to us is full of living power: it is sharper than the sharpest dagger, cutting swift and deep into our innermost thoughts and desires with all their parts, exposing us for what we really are."

Psalms 37:23-24 "The Lord directs the steps of the godly. He delights in every detail of their lives. Though they stumble, they will never fall, for the Lord holds them by the hand".

John 6:33 I have told you these things, so that in me you may have peace, in this world your will have trouble. But take heart! I have overcome the world.

Thoughts on a Page

As you meditate on these scriptures, write down how you plan to use God's word to prepare and conquer your storm.

About the Author:

Taniesha L. Richardson-Wiley enjoys living life to the fullest, and most of all, loves God. Throughout her life, she persevered and worked hard to achieve her goals. Taniesha has been a musician for over 30 years. She was Minister of Music for 12 years at Greater Friendship Missionary Baptist Church, Conway, AR and has been the Minister of Music at Greater Galilee Missionary Baptist Church, Little Rock, AR for 14 years. In this capacity, Taniesha offers leadership and performs within the framework of the church's total ministry. Taniesha also plans the music for the church calendar, incorporates by-laws and rules of discipline and gives musical workshops.

Taniesha served as Music Director of the Middlewestern District (MWD) Baptist Association, Congress of Christian Education, and Youth Advisor of the Youth Obtaining Unity Organization. One of her biggest musical achievements included the production and release of the MWD Live Recording Gospel CD titled, *Power to be Whole*. This live recording occurred in 2007 at the University of Central Arkansas, Snow Fine Arts Performance Hall. Proceeds raised went towards the project as well as the District's Youth Camp.

In addition to her love for music, Taniesha also loves public health. She has been employed at the Arkansas Department of Health (ADH) since 1999 and served in various capacities. She is now a Public Health Section Chief. Prior to this position, Taniesha was the Program Director in the ADH Center for Local Public Health for the ADH In-Person Assister Program and Communities Putting Prevention to Work Program. She was also the Section Chief in the ADH Center for Health Advancement for the ConnectCare Program and School Health Program; Comprehensive Cancer Health Educator, State Distance Learning Coordinator for the ADH Workforce and Career Development Branch and the Federal Program Manager for the ADH Tobacco Prevention and Cessation (Stamp Out Smoking) Branch.

Taniesha offered workshops and presented at statewide trainings and national conferences (Tobacco Use and Prevention, Health Disparities, Sustainability Efforts, Public Health, Interpersonal Communications; Supervisor and Employment Development, ADH Supervision 101, Personal Preparedness for a Pandemic and Other Emergencies, Preparedness 101, ADH BreastCare, Personal and Youth Empowerment and Stress Management).

Taniesha received her Bachelor of Science Degree in Health Education from the University of Central Arkansas, Conway, AR, and her Master of Public Health Degree with an emphasis on Health Policy and Management from the University of Arkansas for Medical Sciences, College of Public Health, Little Rock, AR.

Taniesha served as President of the Arkansas Society for Public Health Education (SOPHE) and committee member of the Arkansas Public Health Association (APHA). She received a

Certificate of Public Health Leadership from the Arkansas Academy for Public Health Leadership, Certificate from the Arkansas Public Health Institute, Certificate of Recognition for Years of Service from the Arkansas Department of Health, and many volunteer awards.

Other achievements include: auditioning and receiving key roles in Christian films; auditioning and being accepted to perform and minister at the Bobbie Jones, *Power to End Stroke Gospel Tour*, and teaching music at R & R Music Studios. In honor of her son and brother, Taniesha relaunched Infinite Melodies Arts and Music, LLC. in 2017 where she teaches youth piano basics, piano technique, and theory. She also enjoyed serving as the Christian Education Director at Greater Galilee Missionary Baptist Church.

Taniesha ultimately enjoys spending time with her family-Kevin and children, Destiny, and Kyler. Her ultimate mission in life is to touch many lives through her ministries and to teach children, youth, and young adults that they can achieve their dreams if they believe and pursue them.

Janiesha's Favorite Scriptures:

Jeremiah 29:11 NIV *"For I know the plans I have for you," declares the Lord, "plans to prosper you and not to harm you, plans to give you hope and a future".*

Proverbs 4:7 *"Wisdom is the principal thing; therefore, get wisdom: and with all thy getting, get understanding".*

Proverbs 3:5-6 *"Trust in the LORD with all thine heart; and lean not unto thine own understanding; in all thy ways acknowledge Him and He will direct thy path".*

Jonah 2:2 *"In my distress, I called to the Lord and he answered me".*

Psalms 91:1 *"He that dwelleth in the secret place of the Highest shall abide under the shadow of the Almighty".*

Psalms 37:2-3 *"Trust in the Lord and do good, then you will live in the land and be secure; if you find your delight in the Lord, he will grant your heart's desires".*

Galatians 5:22 But the fruit of the Spirit is love, joy, peace, forbearance, kindness, goodness, faithfulness.

Taniesha's Final Reflections:

Grateful

I received so many blessings over the years! I must share them so that you can also trust God and understand that He is still in the blessing business, even after the storm or tragic events. I feel even closer to Him than ever before! The closer I am to God, the more at peace I feel! There is a calm in my life and a sense of peace. Even when things are chaotic around you, just whisper "Peace" and exhale. Here are a few of my blessings that I would like to share with you. For these things, I am truly grateful:

A beautiful family- My husband, Kevin, my children- Destiny and Kyler. I thank the Lord for blessing me with Kevin, a man who does not mind working hard to take care of us. He understands his place in our family structure as the head- My prayer is that he follows and submits totally to Christ. As he follows Christ, we are in line to follow him. I am happy once again. It has not always been easy, but to surrender totally to God makes things better and gives me peace. To love again, and to have someone who loves you for who you are- flaws and all, gives me hope. Even after my "relationship storms" over the years, I have learned, and am still learning. It not only feels right, but it is fulfilling. I pray for OUR imperfections, and God hears us and corrects us. I pray for my husband EVERYDAY to continue to follow Christ and listen to His voice. Everything else falls in place when the head follows God.

    I thank God for my daughter Destiny; who is bright and very smart. After teaching her about salvation over a period of time, in 2015, she decided to make Jesus her choice, by accepting Him as her personal Savior at the age of 5. She was baptized on December 6, 2015. Some may say that the age of 5 is too young, but children today are a lot smarter than we were back then! They grasp information a lot quicker and understand the importance of having Christ as the head of their lives. I am reminded of the scripture, "Train up a child in the way that they should go, and when they are old, they will not depart from it". Training starts at home! As parents, we must take out the time with our children instead of letting the world dictate to them what they should do. It is our responsibility to ensure that they receive everything that they need. Now, I am not saying that my child is perfect or will not error, because on her personal journey, she will fall or stumble. The difference is that she will know who to go to when she falls to ask for forgiveness; and how to get back up again. I pray over her life EVERYDAY and will continue to do so as long as I live. I encourage you to do the same over your child or children. Ask God to protect them and as a parent, make sure that you do what you can to protect them. My son Kyler is full of life. I had a tough time getting him here, but I thank God EVERYDAY for him! I also pray over his life that God will watch over him and keep him safe from hurt or harm. As his parents, we dedicated him back to God also on December 6, 2015. We promised God that we will train him up in a Christ-like home and be "examples" before him. This means that we will walk in a way that pleases God so that he will see the right way to live. My prayer is that both of my children grow up having a strong relationship with God. The key: Be an example before your child. When they get older, although they may sway, they will not drift far and will return from your teachings.

Since I began writing this book, I received two promotions on my job. God is able! Yes, I had my financial storms, but now, God has blessed me with enough to not financially struggle anymore. My prayer is that I continue to be a good steward over that which He has blessed me with and to manage my blessings properly. The key: Trusting and Tithing. Now, I have not always done right in this area, but when I did, things were a lot easier! Every year, I strived to do even better in this area. Believe and trust me, this works! When you tithe-CHEERFULLY- giving God 10% of what you earn, the struggle will not be as tough. Watch how God moves in your life and enjoy the "Overflow" of His blessings. He will bless you to be a blessing to others.

I pray that each of you are motivated and inspired; knowing that through it all, God will take care of you and supply you with everything you need. If you do not believe in the power of God, just try Him, and now is the best time to get to know

Him. I could have easily said, if there was a God, he would have saved my first son from dying or He would have healed my brother after his accident, and/or he would have not died. I could have said that if there was a God, innocent children or elderly people in nursing homes would not get abused; or mass shootings would not take place. Those things are not of God. I can go on and on, but I am reminded of this scripture:

"If my people, who are called by my name, will humble themselves and pray and seek my face and turn from their wicked ways, then I will hear from heaven, and I will forgive their sin and will heal their land". 2 Chronicles 7:14.

Our nation needs healing, and it is time that we trust God now more than ever! It is imperative that we turn to Him. When the storms of life are raging, you can stand, because God is your anchor. He will hold onto your hand. It is up to you to not let go of His hand. Whatever storm comes your way, you can make it through it. Stay prepared and connected. I am a witness that He will see you through, give you peace and a calm after your storm; and most of all, He will give you the power to be whole again.

Only through the love of God can you understand life. Reading, thinking, and talking can show the direction to God, but only opening your heart in love and surrender can lead to God. What better way to love God than to love the miracles of all that He has created!" (Reference: What God Wants You to Know)

… Reflections: Thoughts on a Page

Reflections: Thoughts on a Page   Date_____

Reflections: Thoughts on a Page   **Date:** _____

Reflections: Thoughts on a Page   Date_____

Reflections: Thoughts on a Page   Date_____

Reflections: Thoughts on a Page Date_____

Reflections: Thoughts on a Page   Date_____

Reflections: Thoughts on a Page   Date_____

Reflections: Thoughts on a Page   Date_____

Reflections: Thoughts on a Page Date_____

Reflections: Thoughts on a Page   Date_____

Reflections: Thoughts on a Page Date_____

Reflections: Thoughts on a Page   Date_____

Reflections: Thoughts on a Page   Date_____

www.ingramcontent.com/pod-product-compliance
Lightning Source LLC
Chambersburg PA
CBHW060400050426
42449CB00009B/1833